Immigration's Role in Building a Strong American Economy

PRESIDENT BARACK OBAMA DELIVERS REMARKS ON IMMIGRATION REFORM IN THE EAST ROOM OF THE WHITE HOUSE, JUNE 11, 2013. (OFFICIAL WHITE HOUSE PHOTO BY PETE SOUZA)

"So if we're truly committed to strengthening our middle class and providing more ladders of opportunity to those who are willing to work hard to make it into the middle class, we've got to fix the system. We have to make sure that every business and every worker in America is playing by the same set of rules. We have to bring this shadow economy into the light so that everybody is held accountable — businesses for who they hire, and immigrants for getting on the right side of the law. That's common sense. And that's why we need comprehensive immigration reform."

— President Barack Obama, January 29, 2013

America has always been a nation of immigrants, and throughout the nation's history, immigrants from around the globe have kept our workforce vibrant, our businesses on the cutting edge, and helped to build the greatest economic engine in the world. However, America's immigration system is broken and has not kept pace with changing times. Today, too many employers game the system by hiring undocumented workers and there are 11 million people living and working in the shadow economy. Neither is good for the economy or the country. It is time to fix our broken immigration system.

The President has made clear that Democrats, Republicans, and Independents in Congress should work together to enact commonsense immigration reform that includes proposals to continue to strengthen border security, create an earned path to citizenship for undocumented immigrants, hold employers accountable, and bring our legal immigration system into the 21st century. Last month, the Senate passed historic legislation that is largely consistent with the President's principles for commonsense immigration reform with a strong bipartisan vote. The Senate's Border Security, Economic Opportunity and Immigration Modernization Act (S. 744) represents the best chance that our country has had in years to modernize our immigration system. The President urges the House of Representatives to take action and move this bill or similar legislation forward,

1

and stands willing to work with all parties to make sure that commonsense immigration reform becomes a reality as soon as possible.

This report outlines the key benefits to the U.S. economy of passing commonsense immigration reform.

Specifically, the Senate's bipartisan immigration reform bill:

I. **Strengthens the overall economy and grows U.S. GDP:** Independent studies affirm that commonsense immigration reform will increase economic growth. The Congressional Budget Office (CBO) estimated that enacting the Senate immigration reform bill will increase real GDP relative to current law projections by 3.3 percent in 2023 and 5.4 percent in 2033 – an increase of roughly $700 billion in 2023 and $1.4 trillion in 2033 in today's dollars. A larger labor force; higher productivity and investment; and stronger technology, tourism, hospitality, agriculture, and housing industries are just some of the key ways that immigration reform strengthens the U.S. economy.

II. **Fosters innovation and encourages more job creation and job growth in the U.S.:** Evidence shows that immigrants are highly entrepreneurial. Immigration reform would streamline the process for highly-skilled and highly-educated workers to come to the U.S. and build businesses that create jobs for Americans. In addition, it encourages companies to locate, invest, and expand here in the U.S. Under the recently passed Senate legislation, entrepreneurial immigrants would be eligible for newly created temporary and permanent visas if they demonstrate that they have ideas that attract U.S. investment or revenue and establish businesses that create jobs.

III. **Increases the productivity of workers and adds new protections for American workers:** According to CBO and other independent studies, immigration reform will ultimately increase overall U.S. productivity, resulting in higher GDP and higher wages. Part of this gain in productivity comes from immigrants' creating new inventions and companies, as well as from improvements in U.S. production processes. Bringing undocumented workers out of the shadows and into the legal economy also helps put a stop to practices that undercut wages and worsen working conditions for American workers. This bill also has provisions to protect U.S. workers and ensure that new worksite enforcement and border security measures deter future illegal immigration.

IV. **Decreases budget deficits, balances out an aging population, and strengthens Social Security:** The CBO found that the enacting Senate immigration reform bill will reduce the federal budget deficit by nearly $850 billion over the next 20 years. In addition, the independent Chief Actuary of the Social Security Administration (SSA) has found that immigration reform will improve the long-term financial standing of Social Security by adding younger workers to the U.S. workforce. The SSA Actuary estimates that the Senate's immigration reform bill will add nearly $300 billion to the Social Security Trust Fund over the next decade and would improve Social Security's finances over the long run, extending Social Security solvency by two years.

Costs of Inaction

		Costs of Maintaining the Status Quo		Benefits of Comprehensive Immigration Reform
GDP		U.S. economy does not benefit from higher growth, larger workforce, more innovators, entrepreneurs and capital investment, and increased productivity – and domestic production is lower as a result	+	Economy strengthened as U.S. benefits from a larger labor force, higher productivity, and stronger technology, tourism, hospitality, agriculture, and housing industries . In 2033, US economy is 5.4 percent larger than under status quo
Labor force participation		Labor force participation continues to decline as the baby boom generation retires	+	Higher labor force participation than without immigration reform as new working-age immigrants participate in the labor force at a higher rate
Productivity		U.S. workers and capital do not benefit from productivity gains associated with commonsense immigration reform	+	Productivity of labor and capital increases by 1 percent in 2033
Wages		Because workers do not benefit from productivity gains, average wages are lower: a cost of about $250 annually for the median household by 2033 (in today's dollars)	+	Largely as a result of higher productivity, real wages will rise by 0.5 percent in 2033 relative to current law – the equivalent of about an annual $250 increase today for a median household
Protections for U.S. workers		American workers do not benefit from new protections that help ensure immigrants complement the American workforce	+	Employers must recruit U.S. workers for high-skilled occupations; enhanced portability and wage protections for temporary workers; new safeguards against abuses in recruiting foreign labor
Federal deficits		Federal budget does not benefit from additional taxes paid by new and legalizing immigrants – and deficits are nearly $850 billion higher as a result	+	Over the next twenty years, federal deficits are reduced by nearly $850 billion
Federal debt		By 2023, federal debt as a share of the economy is 3 percentage points higher than it would be under immigration reform	+	U.S. debt falls by 3 percentage points as a share of the economy by 2023, compared to current law
Social Security		Social Security does not benefit from new young and healthier workers balancing out retirement of the Baby Boomer generation	+	Extends the solvency of the Social Security Trust Fund by two years and reduces the 75-year shortfall by nearly half a trillion dollars
Entrepreneurship		Talented entrepreneurs are prevented from starting the next set of Fortune 500 companies in the U.S. and patenting new technologies that fuel innovation and provide Americans with well-paying jobs	+	Entrepreneurial immigrants are eligible for newly created temporary and permanent visas if they demonstrate that they have ideas that attract investment and establish businesses that create jobs
Housing		Housing market does not benefit from higher housing demand, delaying the economic revitalization of communities hit hardest by the recession	+	Housing market recovery is strengthened through stronger demand and higher prices for homes in neighborhoods hardest hit by the recession
Tourism and Hospitality		U.S. is unprepared to take advantage of explosive growth in tourism from emerging economies, resulting in fewer tourism and hospitality jobs	+	Provisions in the Senate bill position – including the Visa Waiver Program, new CBP officers, and permanent authorization of the Corporation for Travel Promotion – provide significant boost to these sectors
Agriculture		U.S. agriculture continues to be affected by unpredictable and unstable worker flows, resulting in deportations, employer fines and work stoppages	+	U.S. agricultural output and exports grow over time – supporting a key engine of American economic growth

I.   Strengthening the U.S. Economy and Growing U.S. GDP

IMMIGRATION REFORM WILL BOOST U.S. ECONOMIC GROWTH

❖ **Commonsense immigration reform will lead to greater economic growth by adding more high-demand workers to the labor force, increasing capital investment and overall productivity, and leading to more entrepreneurs starting companies in the U.S.**

   - The bipartisan Senate bill will boost real GDP by 3.3 percent ($700 billion) in 2023 and by 5.4 percent ($1.4 trillion) in 2033, according to CBO.

   - This is enough to boost average annual GDP growth by a projected 0.3 percentage points over the next twenty years.

❖ **Immigration reform will improve U.S. worker and capital productivity, thereby increasing wages for U.S. workers, leading to higher real wages in the long term.**

   - Technological advancements brought by immigrants, such as new inventions and improvements in production processes, also will boost U.S. GDP for years to come.

❖ **Immigration reform provides a boost to sagging labor force participation.**

   - New immigrants of working age are projected to participate in the labor force at a higher rate than native workers, increasing labor force participation rates.

   - The bipartisan Senate bill will increase the labor force by 3.5 percent in 2023 and 5 percent in 2033, according to CBO.

Reforming our broken immigration system will help to grow the economy. According to CBO, commonsense immigration reform will lead to greater economic growth because it will add more high-demand workers to the labor force, increase capital investment and overall productivity, and lead to greater numbers of entrepreneurs starting companies in the U.S. CBO estimates that enacting the bipartisan Senate immigration bill, S. 744, will boost real GDP by 3.3 percent in 2023 and by 5.4 percent in 2033 – an increase of roughly $700 billion in 2023 and $1.4 trillion in 2033 in today's dollars.[1] This is enough to boost average annual projected GDP growth by 0.3 percentage points over the next twenty years.

---

[1] The Congressional Budget Office. "The Economic Impact of S. 744, the Border Security, Economic Opportunity, and Immigration Modernization Act." June 18, 2013. http://www.cbo.gov/publication/44346.

Analysis by former CBO Director and Chief Economist for President George W. Bush's Council of Economic Advisers Douglas Holtz-Eakin also finds that immigration reform will raise the pace of economic growth. In a 2013 American Action Forum report, Holtz-Eakin examines U.S. demographic trends and concludes that immigration reform will increase both near-term economic growth and per capita GDP.[2]

CBO estimates that as a result of the Senate bill, immigrant workers would help increase the productivity of both labor and capital, leading to higher real wages in the long term. CBO also noted that technological advancements brought by immigrants, such as new inventions and improvements in production processes, will boost U.S. GDP for years to come.

One crucial factor in GDP growth is labor force participation, rates of which are projected to decline in the U.S. as the baby boom generation retires. Commonsense immigration reform will significantly boost the national labor force participation rate. Not only will immigration reform increase the population of working-age adults, CBO and the Joint Committee on Taxation project that new immigrants of working age will participate in the labor force at a higher rate, on average, than native workers of working age. Enacting the Senate bill will increase the labor force by 6 million workers, or 3.5 percent, in 2023, and 9 million, or 5 percent, in 2033.[3] According to CBO, higher labor force participation will boost capital investment, which will lead to increased productivity and higher overall average wages.

The following sections explain in more detail how immigrants and the Senate bill in the Senate lead to more American jobs, better productivity and lower federal deficits.

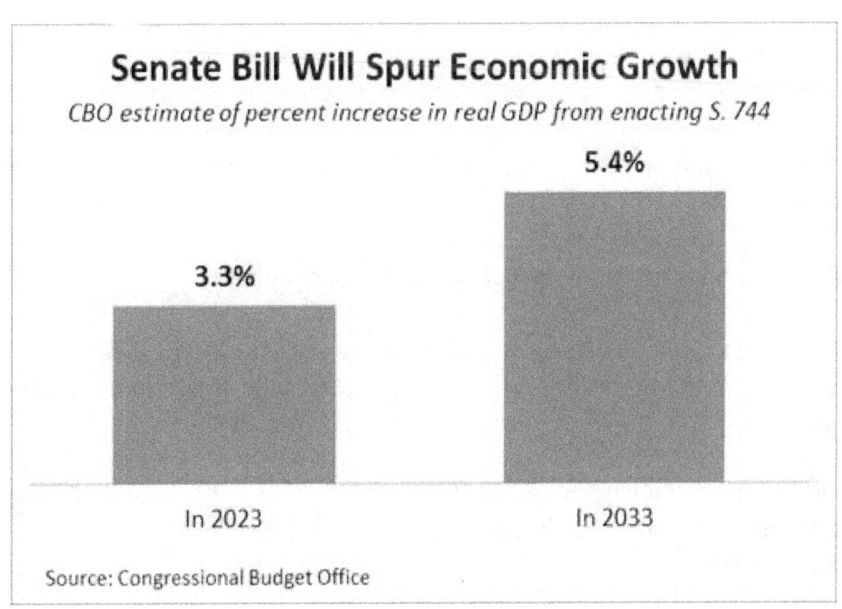

[2] Holtz-Eakin, Douglas. "Immigration Reform, Economic Growth and the Fiscal Challenge." April 2013. http://americanactionforum.org/sites/default/files/Immigration%20and%20the%20Economy%20and%20Budget.pdf.

[3] Congressional Budget Office (June 18, 2013).

II. Fostering Innovation and Encouraging More Job Creation in the U.S.

IMMIGRATION REFORM WILL ENCOURAGE MORE JOB CREATION

❖ **Immigration reform helps U.S. companies attract the most talented workers.**

- The bipartisan Senate bill makes meaningful improvements to the existing employment-based green card system and creates new provisions that strengthen the United States' ability to attract and retain highly-skilled global talent

- Recent studies have shown that immigrants promote productivity and innovation, both directly and indirectly through positive spillover effects on native workers

❖ **Immigration reform attracts entrepreneurs to the U.S. to start companies and create jobs.**

- Immigrant-owned small businesses generated a total of $776 billion in receipts and employed an estimated 4.7 million people in 2007.

- Immigrants started 28 percent of all new U.S. businesses, despite accounting for only 13 percent of the U.S. population in 2011.

- More than 40 percent of Fortune 500 companies were founded by immigrants or children of immigrants. These American companies represent 7 of the 10 most valuable brands globally, collectively employ more than 10 million people and generate annual revenue of $4.2 trillion.

❖ **Immigration reform ensures our nations family-sponsored and employment-based immigration systems complement each other and contribute to economic growth.**

- In choosing a country to move to, prospective immigrants envision a better life not only for themselves but also for their families.

❖ **Immigration reform attracts investments in the U.S. economy.**

- The bipartisan Senate bill reforms and makes permanent the EB-5 immigrant investor program that grants permanent resident status to foreigners who invest above a minimum threshold in new job-creating commercial enterprises in the United States.

- EB-5 investments have been responsible for the infusion of at least $6.8 billion of capital into the United States and the creation of at least 48,950 jobs for U.S. workers as of the end of fiscal year 2012.

Commonsense immigration reform would make it easier for highly-skilled and educated workers and business owners to come to and stay in the U.S. and create jobs, promote innovation, and boost productivity. The bipartisan Senate bill makes meaningful improvements to the existing employment-based green card system and creates new provisions that strengthen the United

States' ability to attract and retain highly-skilled global talent. This includes those who earn advanced degrees in science, technology, engineering, and math (STEM) fields from U.S. universities, and foreign-born entrepreneurs and investors who meet certain criteria.

Impact of Immigrants on Innovation and Worker Productivity

The bipartisan Senate bill eliminates the existing backlogs for employment-based green cards by exempting certain employment-based green cards from limitations on the overall number of such green cards issued each year and by eliminating restrictions on the number of immigrants from populous nations like India and China. It also exempts STEM PhD and Master's graduates from the annual limitations on the amount of green cards available each year. This means, in effect, that STEM graduates with advanced degrees from U.S. colleges and universities and job offers in the U.S. will be able to attain green card status. Taken together, these employment-based green card provisions will boost overall U.S. competitiveness by attracting the world's best and brightest students, employees, and inventors.

An expanding body of contemporary research highlights the contributions to innovation and growth made by immigrants in STEM fields, where development of world-class talent will be critical to America's continued global leadership.[4] The 2010 National Survey of College Graduates, conducted by the National Science Foundation, found that over 60 percent foreign graduate students were enrolled in STEM fields. The study found that although immigrants represent 14 percent of all employed college graduates, they account for 50 percent of PhDs working in math and computer science occupations.[5] Moreover, studies indicate that every foreign-born student with an advanced degree from a U.S. university who stays to work in a STEM field is associated with, on average, 2.6 jobs for American workers.[6]

As described in the 2013 Economic Report of the President, recent studies have shown that immigrants promote productivity and innovation, both directly and indirectly through positive spillover effects on native workers.[7] Researchers have found that immigrants establish patents at twice the rate of U.S.-born citizens.[8] While this largely reflects immigrants' being more heavily represented in science, engineering, and other technical occupations, immigrants in those fields patent at an above average rate even when compared to other non-immigrant scientists and

---

[4] Economic Report of the President. March 2013, p. 156.
http://www.whitehouse.gov/sites/default/files/docs/erp2013/full_2013_economic_report_of_the_president.pdf.

[5] National Science Foundation. National Center for Science and Engineering Statistics (NCSES). "Science and Engineering Indicators 2012." January 2012. http://www.nsf.gov/statistics/seind12/pdf/c02.pdf.

[6] Zavodny, Madeline. American Enterprise Institute and the Partnership for a New American Economy. "Immigration and American Jobs." December 2011. http://www.aei.org/article/society-and-culture/immigration/immigration-and-american-jobs.

[7] Economic Report of the President (March 2013).

[8] Hunt, Jennifer, and Marjolaine Gauthier-Loiselle. "How Much Does Immigration Boost Innovation?" Institute for the Study of Labor (IZA). January 2009. http://ftp.iza.org/dp3921.pdf.

engineers.[9] Additionally, immigrant college graduates are more likely than non-immigrants to have published a scholarly work, and those who had published were more likely to have published six or more scholarly works (6.8 percent of published immigrants compared to 3.6 percent of published native-born graduates).[10]

Increases in high-skilled immigration also have spillover effects that increase the number of patent applications filed by non-immigrants. Jennifer Hunt and Marjolaine Gauthier-Loiselle used a 1940-2000 state panel dataset to show an increase in patents per capita from 9 percent to 18 percent in response to a 1 percentage point increase in immigrant college graduates.[11] High-skilled immigrant students and workers exert a strong, positive impact—both directly and indirectly through spillover effects—on U.S. competitiveness in the global economy.

CBO conducted its own literature review to evaluate the economic impact of the bipartisan Senate bill. Its report concluded, "empirical research broadly suggests that an influx of immigrants, particularly highly skilled immigrants, would lead to increased innovation and task specialization. And those improvements in turn would increase economic output for any given supply of labor and capital stock." From this, CBO determined that the bipartisan Senate bill would boost overall productivity by 0.7 percent in 2023 and by 1 percent in 2033, which would in turn boost GDP per capita, increase wages at all skill levels, and raise the return on investment—improvements that benefit all U.S. workers.[12]

Steve Case, chairman and CEO of Revolution LLC and co-founder of America Online, when testifying before the Senate Judiciary Committee earlier this year, concluded that "high-skilled immigrants have always been job creators, not job takers." He explained, "our success as an entrepreneurial nation is going to be driven largely by our ability to attract and retain the best and brightest talent," including those in high-demand STEM fields.

Supporting Entrepreneurship through Commonsense Immigration Reform

The Senate bill also creates a new Startup or INVEST visa ("Investing in New Venture, Entrepreneurial Startups, and Technologies"). This will allow foreign entrepreneurs who attract a threshold level of financing from U.S. investors or revenue from U.S. customers to build their businesses in the U.S. by creating both temporary visa and permanent green card options for aspiring entrepreneurs. If their companies continue to succeed and create jobs for American workers, these entrepreneurs would be eligible for permanent resident status, and eventually citizenship. Estimates of the economic impact of these provisions vary; however, up to 50,000 jobs

---

[9] Hunt and Gauthier-Loiselle (2009).

[10] Hunt, Jennifer. "Which Immigrants Are Most Innovative and Entrepreneurial? Distinctions by Entry Visa." Journal of Labor Economics. July 2011. http://www.nber.org/papers/w14920.pdf.

[11] Hunt and Gauthier-Loiselle (2009).

[12] The Congressional Budget Office. (June 18, 2013).

could be created each year if all of the green cards established under the parameters of the bill are utilized.[13]

Commonsense immigration reform will expand the type of entrepreneurship and young growing firms that disproportionately contribute to the dynamism of the economy. Many immigrants are highly entrepreneurial, starting new businesses that fuel job creation and contribute to economic dynamism and growth. A 2010 paper by economists from the University of Maryland and the U.S. Census Bureau found that startups created almost 3.5 million net non-farm jobs in 2005: the authors concluded that startups accounted for only 3 percent of employment but almost 20 percent of gross job creation.[14]

A study by the Fiscal Policy Institute found that in 2007, immigrant-owned small businesses generated a total of $776 billion in receipts and employed an estimated 4.7 million people.[15] According to the 2012 Kauffman Index of Entrepreneurial Activity, immigrants were nearly twice as likely as U.S.-born citizens to start new businesses each month. The immigrant rate of entrepreneurship increased from 2005 to 2012, while the native-born rate has remained flat over the past 17 years. For immigrants, 490 out of 100,000 immigrants started a business each month, compared with 260 out of 100,000 people for the native-born.[16]

In a 2012 report, the Partnership for a New American Economy found that in 2011, immigrants started 28 percent of all new U.S. businesses, despite accounting for only 12.9 percent of the U.S. population; by contrast, in 1996, only 15 percent of new U.S. businesses were founded by immigrants.[17] In the decade from 1990 to 2000, the number of immigrant small business owners grew by 540,000, accounting for 30 percent of the total growth in the number of people who own a small business over that period.[18]

---

[13] Based on the parameters of Border Security, Economic Opportunity, and Immigration Modernization Act of 2013. S. 744. 113th Congress.

[14] Haltiwanger, John C., Ron S. Jarmin, and Javier Miranda. "Who Creates Jobs? Small vs. Large vs. Young." NBER Working Paper No. 16300. February, 2012. http://www.nber.org/papers/w16300.pdf?new_window=1.

[15] Kallick, David D. "Immigrant Small Business Owners: A Significant and Growing Part of the Economy." Fiscal Policy Institute. 2012. http://fiscalpolicy.org/wp-content/uploads/2012/06/immigrant-small-business-owners-FPI-20120614.pdf.

[16] Fairlie, Robert. "Kauffman Index of Entrepreneurial Activity: 1996–2012." The Ewing Marion Kauffman Foundation. April, 2013. http://www.kauffman.org/uploadedFiles/KIEA_2013_report.pdf.

[17] Partnership for a New American Economy (2012).

[18] Kallick, David D. "Immigrant Small Business Owners: A Significant and Growing Part of the Economy." Fiscal Policy Institute. 2012. http://fiscalpolicy.org/wp-content/uploads/2012/06/immigrant-small-business-owners-FPI-20120614.pdf.

Immigrants' contributions in the high-tech sector are especially striking, both in the number of businesses started and in the number of patents filed, as discussed above. In 2005, over 50 percent of new tech startups in Silicon Valley—widely known as the international hub for technological development and innovation—had at least one immigrant founder.[19] One study notes that immigrants started 25 percent of all engineering and technology companies founded between 1995 and 2005.[20]

However, some new research suggests the U.S. is losing its competitive edge in retaining immigrant entrepreneurs. The Kauffman Foundation reports that the number of Silicon Valley startups with at least one immigrant co-founder fell by over 8 percent, from 52 percent for companies founded between 1995 and 2005, to 44 percent for companies founded between 2006 and 2012. They attribute this notable drop to a "reverse brain drain," wherein highly-skilled workers are leaving the U.S., and returning home or to other countries.[21] The Senate bill's increase of employment-based green cards, especially for STEM PhD and Master's graduates, will

---

[19] Wadhwa, Vivek, AnnaLee Saxenian, Ben Rissing, and Gary Gereffi. "America's New Immigrant Entrepreneurs." report by the Duke School of Engineering and the UC Berkeley School of Information. January 4, 2007. http://people.ischool.berkeley.edu/~anno/Papers/Americas_new_immigrant_entrepreneurs_I.pdf.

[20] Wadhwa, Saxenian, Rissing, and Gereffi (2007).

[21] Wadhwa, Saxenian, Rissing, and Gereffi (2007).

provide highly skilled foreign students, employees, and inventors a greater opportunity to remain in the U.S. as permanent residents and eventually as U.S. citizens.

At the other end of the spectrum, immigrants have also created—and continue to build—many of the world's largest and best-known companies. More than 40 percent of Fortune 500 companies were founded by immigrants or children of immigrants. These American companies, including Google, Disney, and Procter & Gamble, to name a few, represent 7 of the 10 most valuable brands globally. They collectively employ more than 10 million people worldwide and generate annual revenue of $4.2 trillion.[22]

Increasing Investment Through Commonsense Immigration Reform

The bipartisan Senate bill reforms and makes permanent the EB-5 immigrant investor program that grants permanent resident status to foreigners who invest above a minimum threshold in new job-creating commercial enterprises in the United States. Since the program was created in 1990,

---

[22] Partnership for a New American Economy, "The New American Fortune 500," June 2011, http://www.renewoureconomy.org/sites/all/themes/pnae/img/new-american-fortune-500-june-2011.pdf.

EB-5 investments have been responsible for the infusion of at least $6.8 billion of capital into the United States and the creation of at nearly 50,000 jobs for U.S. workers as of the end of fiscal year 2012. Under current law, immigrants must invest a minimum of $1,000,000 in a new or existing U.S. business or project, or a minimum of $500,000 if the business or project is located in a Targeted Employment Area (an area which, at the time of investment, is experiencing an unemployment rate of at least 150% of the national average) or a rural area. The investment must either create or preserve a minimum of 10 full time jobs for qualifying U.S. workers within two years.

The bipartisan Senate bill would increase the number of immigrant investor visas available each year through the aforementioned reforms to the employment-based immigration system, and add additional measures to encourage more investment in areas that are most in need of economic development. Overall, these reforms have the potential to support more than 140,000 jobs for American workers each year.[23] In short, immigration reform will attract more foreign investment to the U.S. that will catalyze economic development and create jobs.

Family-Sponsored Immigration as Support for Critical Workers

The prospect of family reunification has been a cornerstone of U.S. immigration policy throughout our nation's history. The Senate bill reforms and begins to eliminate the backlog in the family-sponsored immigration system by exempting immediate family members (spouses and unmarried children under the age of 21) of lawful permanent residents from the annual limitations on family-sponsored green cards and by increasing the limit on the number of immigrants allowed each year from individual countries, including those nations with a high rate of immigration such as China, India, Mexico, and the Philippines. The Senate bill also excludes these same immediate family members from annual limitations on employment-based green cards, and removes annual country limitations altogether from this system.

Contrary to some assertions by opponents of immigration reform, our nation's family-sponsored and employment-based immigration systems are equally important and complement each other in many ways. In choosing their new home, prospective immigrants envision a better life not only for themselves but also for their families. Using data arranged by year of arrival and country of origin, one study found a positive correlation between the fraction of immigrants sponsored by a sibling and average education levels of the immigrants. The data seem to support the notion that highly educated immigrants who arrive based on employment and occupational preference categories then sponsor their siblings who are also highly educated.[24]

---

[23] The exemptions for spouses and dependents on the worldwide cap will result in approximately 14,000 green cards being available each year for individual immigrant investors. Since the Senate bill maintains current law requirements that a minimum of 10 jobs must be created or preserved for each EB-5 investment, these reforms could support more than 140,000 jobs for American workers each year.

[24] Duleep, Harriet O., and Mark C. Regets. 1996. "Family Unification, Siblings, and Skills." In Immigrants and Immigration Policy: Individual Skills, Family Ties, and Group Identities, edited by Harriet Duleep and Phanindra Wunnava, pp. 219–44. Greenwich, CT: JAI Press.

Family-sponsored immigration has significant economic benefits, especially for long-term economic growth. According to the National Foundation for American Policy, family-sponsored immigration supports the establishment and operation of small businesses in the United States.[25] For example, Yahoo! Co-founder Jerry Yang came to the U.S. at age 10 with his family. It is also important to realize that immigrants who come through our humanitarian visa system fleeing persecution are also some of our greatest entrepreneurs. Take someone like Sergey Brin – his family fled the Soviet Union when he was a young boy. America welcomed Sergey and his family as refugees, and in return, he went onto co-found Google. The Senate bill also includes provisions that will strengthen existing humanitarian visa programs.

It is clear that a robust family-sponsored immigration system and generous humanitarian visa program are both critical for providing support to family members in the workforce and unleashing entrepreneurial activities, which ultimately is in the best interest of all Americans.

---

[25] Anderson, Stuart. "Family Immigration: The Long Wait to Immigrate." National Foundation for American Policy, Policy Brief. May 2010: 7. http://www.nfap.com/pdf/0505brief-family-immigration.pdf.

III. Increasing the Productivity of U.S. Workers and Strengthening Protections for American Workers

Impact of Immigrants on Productivity and Wages

As discussed above, higher immigration increases U.S. workers' productivity by contributing to technological advancement. These increases in worker productivity mean higher wages, on

14

average. Researchers have also found that immigrants increase the productivity of U.S. workers by complementing their skills.

The recent CBO analysis is clear that, in the long run, the Senate bill raises wages for all groups of workers by boosting productivity. Specifically, CBO estimates that real wages will be 0.5 percent higher in 2033 than projected under current law. In today's terms, that would be equivalent to an additional $250 of income for the median American household. This is largely the result of the increases in productivity of both labor and capital: CBO estimates the Senate bill will increase total factor productivity by 0.7 percent in 2023 and 1 percent in 2033.

A number of careful studies have attempted to isolate the wage impact of immigration among native workers. In particular, economists have used a number of natural experiments – including Cuban immigration to Miami, immigration flows to California in the 1990s and 2000s, and immigration of Russian Jews to Israel in the 1990s – to study the effects of immigration on labor markets. They have generally found that increased immigration raises average wages of U.S.-born workers and has little or no effect on wages even for low-skilled workers, and may have positive effects. The logic behind the empirical finding that immigration has little impact on wages for U.S.-born workers is that immigrants may mostly complement rather than substitute for these workers.

One of the most famous and well-regarded studies in this area is by David Card at the University of California-Berkeley. Using a natural experiment – the experience of the Miami labor market following the arrival of 125,000 Cuban immigrants between May and September 1980, which increased the labor force by 7 percent – Card evaluates the effect of unskilled immigration on the labor market opportunities of native workers.[26] Specifically, he compared the trends in Miami wages to similar cities across the country where this influx did not occur. He finds that a 7 percent increase in the Miami labor market of low-skilled immigrants had virtually no effect on the wage rates or unemployment rate of low-skilled non-Cuban workers. His data analysis suggests a remarkably rapid absorption of the new immigrants into the Miami labor force with negligible effects on other groups. Average wages for natives rose by 0.6 percent and there was essentially no effect or even a small positive effect on wages of the least-educated workers. Economists Rachel Friedberg from Brown University and Jennifer Hunt from Rutgers have conducted similar studies and reached similar results to Card.[27]

Other recent studies also have found that immigration can indeed have positive effects on native wages. For example, Giovanni Peri studies immigration to California over the 1990 to 2004 period. Although he finds negative effects on the wages of other recent immigrants, he finds positive

[26] Card, David. "The Impact of the Mariel Boatlift on the Miami Labor Market." Industrial and Labor Relations Review. January 1990. http://davidcard.berkeley.edu/papers/mariel-impact.pdf.

[27] Friedberg, Rachel. "The Impact of Mass Migration on the Israeli Labor Market." Quarterly Journal of Economics. 2001. http://qje.oxfordjournals.org/content/116/4/1373.full.pdf+html; Hunt, Jennifer. "The Impact of the 1962 Repatriates from Algeria on the French Labor Market." Industrial & Labor Relations Review. April 1992. http://www.jstor.org/stable/2524278.

wage effects for native workers.[28] Peri's most conservative estimate finds immigration yields a net wage benefit to natives of 2.2 percent on average; his study's median estimate finds that immigrants spurred wage growth of native U.S. workers by approximately 4 percent.

One reason that immigrants would not reduce the wages of native workers, and may even increase wages, is that they are not perfect substitutes for American workers. The most commonly cited study that supports the view that immigrants reduce wages is by George Borjas[29], whose research method assumes that immigrants and natives are substitutes for one another. He looks at inflows of immigrants across different schooling levels over time and compares those changes in inflows to changes in the wages of similarly educated natives. However, if immigrants and natives of similar schooling levels are not substitutable, as much of the research suggests, then Borjas' research overstates the negative impact on wages. Additionally, if other factors are also acting to decrease wages for low-skilled native workers, such as technological changes and the decrease of unionized workplaces, then the negative effects may also be overstated.

As previously mentioned, there is a growing body of recent research that suggests that the skills and talents that immigrants and natives bring to the labor market may not be good substitutes for each other, and that low-skilled immigrants may instead enhance the productivity of even low-skilled natives. As Cato Institute scholar Daniel Griswold noted in 2011 testimony before the House Judiciary Committee, "[I]mmigrants tend to bring a different set of skills and differing preferences for the kind of work they perform compared to native-born workers, which means immigrants are less easily substituted for their native-born counterparts."[30] In particular, rather than replacing U.S. workers or reducing U.S. workers' wages, increases in the number of new immigrants lead U.S. workers to specialize in tasks requiring stronger English language and other skills, raising their earnings.[31] One recent Immigration Policy Center study on the impact of recent immigrants in the U.S. labor force evaluated U.S. Census data and found that "there is little apparent relationship between recent immigration and unemployment rates among African Americans, or any other native-born racial/ethnic group, at the state or metropolitan level."[32]

---

[28] Peri, Giovanni. "Immigrants Complementarities and Native Wages: Evidence from California." NBER Working Paper 12956. March 2007. http://www.nber.org/papers/w12956.

[29] Borjas, George. "The Labor Demand Curve is Downward Sloping: Reexamining the Impact of Immigration on the Labor Market." The Quarterly Journal of Economics. November 2003. http://www.hks.harvard.edu/fs/gborjas/publications/journal/QJE2003.pdf.

[30] Griswold, Daniel. "ICE Worksite Enforcement – Up to the Job?" Testimony before the House Committee on the Judiciary Subcommittee on Immigration Policy and Enforcement. January 26, 2011. http://judiciary.house.gov/hearings/pdf/Griswold01262011.pdf.

[31] Peri, Giovanni, and Chad Sparber. "Task Specialization, Immigration, and Wages." American Economic Journal: Applied Economics. 2009.

[32] Immigration Policy Center. "Immigration and Native-Born Unemployment across Racial/Ethnic Groups: Untying the Knot, Part II of II." May 2009. www.immigrationpolicy.org/sites/default/files/docs/Part%202%20-%20Unemployment%20Race%20Disconnect%2005-19-09.pdf.

In its economic analysis of the bipartisan Senate bill, CBO found that in the short-run, wages for some groups of workers will increase modestly while wages for other groups could fall modestly under the Senate bill, and predicted a small and temporary negative adjustment in the overall average wage. But as CBO explains, its analysis does not separately consider the effects on U.S. and foreign-born workers – meaning that this "do[es] not necessarily imply that current U.S. residents would be worse off." In fact, as CBO notes, the temporary reduction in average wages is at least partly attributable to an increase in lower-wage immigrants: because new immigrants would, on average, earn lower wages than the current workforce, their entry into the labor force would reduce the overall average wage to a small degree. Additionally, as noted above, CBO finds that over the long run – once productivity gains and higher capital levels materialize – all skill groups would see higher wages as a result of enacting the Senate bill, with real wages rising by the equivalent of $250 annually for the median household, in today's dollars.

Commonsense immigration reform will also increase wages and productivity for immigrants themselves. One reason that people seek to immigrate to the United States is that they can earn higher wages working in the U.S. than in their home countries. They also have greater opportunities to start businesses and pursue an education. Moreover, by providing a path to earned citizenship, the Senate bill will also give undocumented immigrants the security they need to invest in their own skills and education and to change employers or jobs in pursuit of higher-paying employment, or to stand up for their legal rights if they are paid substandard wages. Studies of the 1986 immigration reform law found that legalizing immigrants saw wage gains in the range of 10 percent as a result of obtaining legal status. Part of this increase reflected increases in workers' productivity, which benefits the economy as a whole.[33]

Protections for American Workers

The Senate's immigration bill includes additional protections for American workers that help ensure immigrants will complement the American workforce and make our economy more productive and competitive. One critical protection is the requirement that employers first recruit American workers before hiring high-skilled temporary foreign workers. At the same time, the bill strengthens prohibitions against displacing American workers and requires that employers pay fair market wages to temporary workers, which helps to prevent American workers from being undercut by cheaper labor. The Department of Labor would also receive new tools and abilities to crack down on employers who fail to comply with the law.

These new safeguards advance the effort to ensure that highly-skilled temporary immigrant workers do not take jobs from equally qualified U.S. workers. Instead, temporary workers would be able to help fill critical skills gaps in the U.S. economy, making American businesses more productive and competitive at home and abroad.

---

[33] See for example, Sherrie A. Kossoudji and Deborah Cobb-Clark. "Coming Out of the Shadows: Learning about Legal Status and Wages from the Legalized Population." Journal of Labor Economics. July 2002.

The Senate bill also introduces additional measures in temporary worker programs to provide immigrant workers with increased mobility and key labor protections so that they are not taken advantage of by unscrupulous employers. A 2010 Center for American Progress study found that "the wages of native-born workers also increase under the comprehensive immigration reform scenario because the 'wage floor' rises for all workers—particularly in industries where large numbers of easily exploited, low-wage, unauthorized immigrants currently work."[34]

Creating a pathway to earned citizenship — in and of itself — will raise the workplace standards for all workers. When immigrants enjoy the same workplace protections and economic mobility as others, they will be less subject to exploitation at the hands of employers whose practices undermine the wages and working conditions of all other workers. The bipartisan Senate bill protects vulnerable immigrant workers from exploitation through strong new prohibitions against labor recruiting and trafficking abuses. And the bill also ensures that all workers have access to the same labor and employment protections regardless of immigration status, so some employers cannot seek out undocumented workers for the purposes of paying lower wages and benefits. For example, under the bill, if an employer hires an undocumented worker and commits a labor violation, not only is that employer subject to higher penalties, but the worker can temporarily stay in the country if he or she agrees to work with the government to investigate the employer. These provisions will protect American workers by removing incentives to seek out and hire undocumented workers.

Immigration reform also makes it easier for employers to comply with the law and deters future undocumented immigration. Commonsense measures, such as mandating that every employer in the country use E-Verify, an electronic employment verification system to ensure that the workers they hire are in the U.S. legally and authorized to work, both establish a more transparent worksite and help to hold employers accountable for knowingly hiring undocumented workers. This will protect businesses that play by the rules and invest in American workers. Additionally, increased investments in border security, on top of the historic investments already made by the Administration over the past four years, will also deter future undocumented immigration. Combined, these efforts will allow more Americans and legal immigrants to secure well paying, middle class jobs, and ensure that U.S. companies continue to the have access to the most talented workforce in the world.

Unleashing Immigrants' Full Economic Potential

Commonsense immigration reform would improve productivity and boost economic growth by increasing various types of investment, including investments not currently made by undocumented workers.

---

[34] The Center for American Progress. "Raising the Floor for American Workers: The Economic Benefits of Comprehensive Immigration Reform." January 2010. http://www.americanprogress.org/wp-content/uploads/2012/09/immigrationeconreport3.pdf.

Investment takes place when one expends resources today, whether in the form of time or money, in the expectation of a greater return in the future. Education is a form of investment. Of course, students do not typically earn much while in school, but they pursue higher education expecting that, in the future, they will earn a higher return, or a better living, as a result. Putting time or money into starting a business is another form of investment. New businesses rarely earn significant revenue in their first year or two, but their owners press on, expecting the enterprise to grow and generate profits over time. As with entrepreneurship, it is this type of investment and risk-taking that has made the American economy as strong as it is today.

When individuals are insecure and uncertain about their position in the economy — whether they are living in the shadows, afraid to enforce basic rights, or unsure if they will be able to stay in the U.S.— their incentives and ability to make such investments is undermined. Individuals may be less inclined to save or invest money today, or to spend on education now, if they doubt that they will be able to enjoy the benefits of such investments in the future.

This is another reason why immigration reform is so important for the economy. When workers avoid investing due to uncertainty about their future, it decreases capital available for all Americans. When immigrants feel they can't invest in their own education or in the education of their children, it hurts the quality of our workforce.

On a related note, research tells us that children whose parents obtain legal status do better in school are more likely to stay in school than children whose parents are undocumented.[35] An estimated 80 percent of children with one or more undocumented parents are already US citizens, and the vast majority of these children will be in the US for the rest of their lives.[36] Enacting bipartisan immigration reform and providing the chance for their parents to come out of the shadows could mean significantly better outcomes for our children, strengthening our future workforce and contributing more to economic growth.

The bipartisan Senate bill would offer a tough but fair pathway for earned citizenship to the 11 million undocumented workers living and working in our communities—a pathway that requires passing background checks, learning English, paying taxes and a penalty, and then going to the back of the line behind everyone who's playing by the rules and trying to come here legally. It also provides farmworkers, who help harvest our nation's fruits and vegetables, with a unique pathway to earned citizenship, if they continue to contribute to the agriculture industry. Finally, the Senate bill would provide an expedited path to permanent status for young people known as DREAMers

---

[35] See Frank D. Bean, Mark A. Leach, Susan K. Brown, and James Bachmeier. "Mexican Immigrant Legalization and Naturalization and Children's Economic Well-Being." In: *Helping Young Refugees and Immigrants Succeed* (eds. Gerhard Sonnert and Gerald Holton), Palgrave Macmillan, New York, 2010; and Ying Pan. "Gains from Legality: Parents Immigration Status and Children's Scholastic Achievement." Working Paper No. 2011–05, Department of Economics, Louisiana State University, 2011, http://bus.lsu.edu/McMillin/Working_Papers/pap11_05.pdf

[36] Passell, Jeffrey S. and D'Vera Cohen. 2010. *Unauthorized Immigrant Population: National and State Trends,* 2010. Washington, DC: Pew Hispanic Center, February. http://www.pewhispanic.org/files/reports/133.pdf

— those who were brought to the U.S. as children and grew up pledging allegiance to our flag and are either attending college or have served honorably in the U.S. military.

IV. Decreasing Budget Deficits, Balancing Out an Aging Population, and Strengthening Social Security

IMMIGRATION WILL CUT THE DEFICIT AND STRENGTHEN SOCIAL SECURITY

❖ **Immigration reform improves the short- and long-term federal budget outlook**

- The additional taxes paid by new and legalizing immigrants would not only offset any new spending, but would be substantial enough to reduce the deficit over the 20-year window.

- Over the twenty years between 2014 and 2033, the Senate bill would reduce federal deficits by nearly $850 billion.

❖ **Immigration reform helps balance out an aging population and shore up U.S. social insurance programs**

- Because most immigrants are young, additional immigration helps balance out the increase in retirees-per-worker that will occur as the Baby Boomer generation retires, and thus provide essential financial support for U.S. social insurance programs.

- Enacting the Senate immigration reform bill will add nearly $300 billion to the Social Security Trust Fund over the next decade—reducing the Social Security shortfall by nearly half a trillion dollars over the next 75 years (0.21 percent of taxable payroll), and extending the life of the Trust Fund by two years.

- Immigrants contribute more to the Medicare Trust Fund then they collect in benefits, according to one study.

Impact of Commonsense Immigration Reform on Budget Deficits and Debt

Along with growing our economy through increases in productivity and more entrepreneurship and innovation, commonsense immigration reform will reduce federal deficits and strengthen Social Security by balancing out an aging population. On net, the Senate-passed bill would reduce federal budget deficits by $158 billion and increase real U.S. GDP by 3.3 percent by 2023. By 2033, CBO estimates that immigration reform will lead to even bigger reductions in federal deficits: in the second decade after enactment, from 2024-2033, the Senate bill would achieve about $700 billion in net deficit reduction. Therefore, over the twenty years between 2014 and 2033, the Senate bill would reduce federal deficits by nearly $850 billion.

The CBO analysis made clear that the additional taxes paid by new and legalizing immigrants would not only offset any new spending, but would be substantial enough to reduce the deficit over the 20-year window. As CBO explains, a significant portion of the new taxes would be paid by previously undocumented immigrants who could earn legal status over time. While many of these workers already pay federal taxes, millions more will pay payroll taxes once they are able to obtain legal status and work above board.[37]

The resulting deficit reduction will also help to reduce our debt as a share of the economy. Economists and budget experts agree that our fiscal goals should include putting our debt on a declining path as a share of our economy. The bipartisan Senate bill helps us toward our goal of fiscal sustainability: looking at CBO's official estimate of the deficit reduction resulting from the Senate immigration reform bill together with CBO's analysis of the impact of the Senate bill on GDP growth, the Senate bill would reduce the federal debt as a share of the economy by three percentage points in 2023, relative to current law. And based on further analysis of the CBO estimates, by 2033, enacting the Senate bill would reduce federal debt by seven percentage points, as a share of the economy compared to current law.

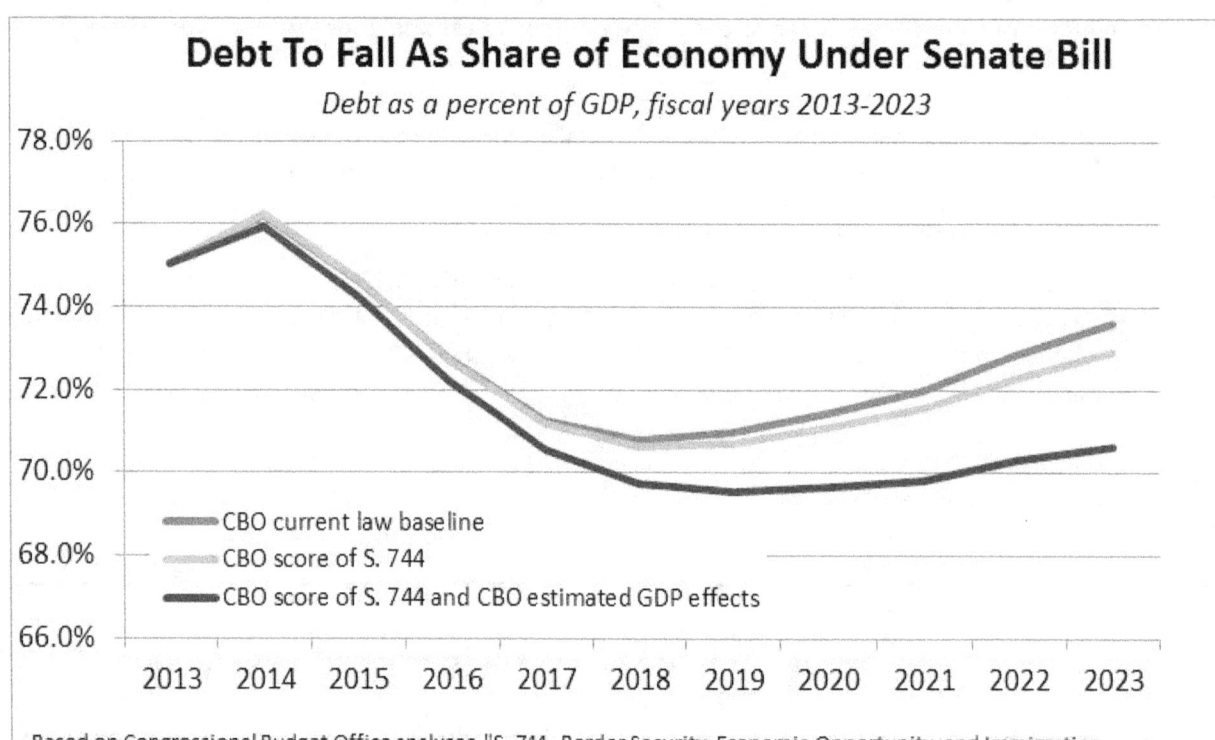

Based on Congressional Budget Office analyses "S. 744, Border Security, Economic Opportunity, and Immigration Modernization Act: As Passed by the Senate on June 27, 2013," "The Economic Impact of S. 744, the Border Security, Economic Opportunity, and Immigration Modernization Act," and "Updated Budget Projections: Fiscal Years 2013 to 2023," May 2013. Debt under S. 744 (assuming the Senate immigration reform bill is enacted) is based on the CBO estimate of net deficit reduction ($158 billion from FY 2014-23) as well as the estimated savings in debt-service costs that would result.

The CBO score reflects the direct impact of immigration reform on the U.S. population, employment, and taxable compensation, and CBO also notes that immigration reform will significantly impact the economy in ways beyond direct changes in the workforce.[38] Immigration

---

[37] The Congressional Budget Office (June 18, 2013) and "S. 744, Border Security, Economic Opportunity, and Immigration Modernization Act: As Passed by the Senate on June 27, 2013." July 2013, http://cbo.gov/publication/44397.

[38] The Congressional Budget Office (June 18, 2013).

reform is expected to bolster the U.S. economy by increasing productivity, driving up overall wages, and boosting the return on investment. Although indirect feedback effects are (appropriately) not incorporated in CBO's official budget estimates, CBO noted that these estimated changes in productivity, wages, and investment from the Senate bill would likely reduce the deficit by an additional $300 billion between 2024 and 2033, on top of the approximately $850 billion in deficit reduction included in the official CBO score.

Impact of Commonsense Immigration Reform on Social Security

Immigration reform will also help secure the financial future of Social Security by increasing immigrants' contributions to the Social Security Trust Fund through payroll taxes.

The independent Office of the Chief Actuary at the Social Security Administration (SSA) reported that enacting the bipartisan Senate immigration reform bill will strengthen Social Security over the long term and extend the life of the Trust Fund by two years, from 2033 to 2035.[39] According to the SSA Actuary, commonsense immigration reform would add nearly $300 billion to the Social Security Trust Fund over the next decade and reduce the Social Security shortfall by nearly half a trillion dollars over the next 75 years in present value terms (equivalent to 0.21 percent of taxable payroll). The reduction in the shortfall is enough of an improvement to nearly reverse the deterioration in Social Security's finances due to the economic downturn.[40]

The bipartisan Senate bill would provide the opportunity for undocumented immigrants to come out of the shadows, obtain documents that will permit them to work above board, and pay taxes like everyone else.   As documented workers, these undocumented immigrants would pay significantly more in federal taxes as a result – on top of the billions of dollars in federal, state, and local taxes that they already currently pay. The Senate bill also modifies legal immigration limits and classifications to increase the U.S. population by 15 million by 2033. Compared to current U.S. citizens, immigrants are on average younger, healthier and have higher than average labor force participation rates. These new immigrants will join the American workforce and pay U.S. payroll and other taxes.

Because most immigrants are young, additional immigration will increase the ratio of workers to retirees. The infusion of young, healthy workers into the formal U.S. economy will help to balance out the otherwise aging U.S. population and provide essential financial support for U.S. social insurance programs. The retirement of the Baby Boomer generation makes this especially timely

---

[39] Office of the Chief Actuary, Social Security Administration. "Response to The Honorable Marco Rubio's request for estimates of the financial effects on Social Security of S. 744, the 'Border Security, Economic Opportunity, and Immigration Modernization Act.'" June 28, 2013. http://www.ssa.gov/OACT/solvency/MRubio_20130627.pdf.

[40] Based on the Social Security Trustees Reports for 2009-2011. Between 2008 and 2011, revisions in the projected actuarial balance due to the economic downturn totaled approximately 0.25 percent of taxable payroll, compared to the 0.21 percentage point improvement that would result from enactment of the Senate immigration reform bill. See table IV.B9. and related text in each Trustees Report for more detail.

and important. The large number of Baby Boomer retirees that will enroll in Social Security and Medicare over the next two decades will create a significant financial strain on these essential programs. The new additions to the formal U.S. workforce will help counteract this trend.

Similarly, Harvard Medical School researchers found that immigrants contribute more to the Medicare Trust Fund then they collect in benefits.[41] Their study, recently published in Health Affairs, concluded that: "Encouraging a steady flow of young immigrants would help offset the aging of the U.S. population and the health care financing challenge that it presents."

The evidence shows that immigration reform will reduce U.S. federal budget deficits, raise labor force participation, and provide financial support for U.S. social insurance programs just as the economy and the budget are coming come under increased strain from the retirement of the Baby Boomer generation. Adding younger and healthier immigrants with high workforce participation rates is critical to U.S. fiscal health in the long-term.

---

[41] Zallman, Leah, Steffie Woolhandler, David Himmelstein, David Bor, and Danny McCormick. "Immigrants Contributed An Estimated $115.2 Billion More To The Medicare Trust Fund Than They Took Out in 2002-2009." Health Affairs. May 2013.

V. Immigration Reform Benefits the Economy across Sectors

In addition to the benefits described above – increasing total economic growth, boosting worker productivity, increasing innovation, and strengthening our fiscal health – the bipartisan Senate bill would bring specific benefits to a range of economic sectors, including agriculture, tourism and hospitality, and housing.

Strengthening America's Housing Recovery

Immigrants are a crucial factor in the United States' housing recovery. A recent study from the Americas Society/Council for the Americas and Partnership for a New American Economy found that the 40 million immigrants currently in the U.S. have created $3.7 trillion in housing wealth. Moreover, immigrants help boost property values by increasing the demand for housing, as well as for other locally produced goods and services. Albert Saiz has found that an immigrant inflow equal to 1 percent of a city's population is associated with a 1 percent increase in home prices in that city.[42]

Immigrants stabilize and revitalize communities facing declining home values, encouraging other middle- and working-class Americans to move to and settle in these communities. Immigrants revitalize less desirable peripheral neighborhoods in costly metropolitan areas by moving into these harder hit neighborhoods, driving demand through their own purchasing power, and then drawing U.S.-born individuals to these areas. Research has shown, for example, that immigration has stemmed the decline of Rust Belt cities and rural areas. For example, the average home in Gary, Indiana, saw an estimated $1,500 increase in value due to the approximately 13,000 immigrants that have settled there since 1990. Moreover, the largest impacts of immigration on the housing market have been seen in areas hardest hit by the recession. In many Sunbelt cities, the direct and indirect effects of immigration over the last 10 years have contributed over $10,000 to the value of the typical home, mitigating the recession's impact on hardest hit states like Arizona and New Mexico.

Immigration reform will further improve the housing market by: enabling more immigrants to achieve homeownership by building credit and other documentation needed for mortgage; boosting immigrant incomes, which will in turn drive housing demand through immigrants' growing purchasing power; and increasing the number of US residents by 10.4 million by 2023, according to the CBO estimate, in part by facilitating family reunification and household formation.

Promoting American Agriculture

---

[42] Saiz, Albert. "Immigration and Housing Rents in American Cities." Journal of Urban Economics. 2007. realestate.wharton.upenn.edu/research/papers/full/433.pdf.

The agriculture industry – a key engine of American economic growth – is especially reliant on immigrant workers. Currently, the agriculture industry is hampered by a broken immigration system that fails to produce predictable and stable worker flows. Today, roughly half of all farmworkers are estimated to be unauthorized[43], which means deportations, employer fines, and work stoppages are a constant fear. Moreover, there continue to be insufficient U.S. workers to fill labor needs: of those crop workers surveyed between 2007 and 2009, 71 percent were foreign born.[44]

Often, farmers and ranchers have difficulty securing laborers for critical tasks. For example, due to our broken immigration system, the state of Georgia experienced a shortage of more than 11,000 agricultural workers in the spring 2011. A recent survey of fruit and vegetable producers in that state identified an economic loss of $181 million and 1,500 fewer jobs in agriculture and related industries due to labor-related production losses. That survey represented a little less than half of total Georgia production acreage; the study noted that if its results were representative of all acreage, the total yearly impact would be about $390 million and the job loss would be about 3,250 on a statewide basis.[45]

In New York, analysis by the Farm Credit Associations found that over 800 farms would be at risk of closure if immigrant labor severely contracted.[46] Without immigrant labor, agricultural operations across the country – including apple farmers in Washington, citrus processors in Florida, and strawberry, raisin, asparagus, and lettuce growers in California – would be forced to cut jobs, raise prices, or succumb to foreign competition.[47] If agriculture's access to migrant labor were cut off, short-term production losses would measure between $5 billion and $9 billion per year.[48]

To bring rationality and predictability to this broken system, the bipartisan Senate bill would replace the H-2A visa with two new guest worker visas: one for agricultural workers with a written contract for employment (W-3) and one for agricultural workers with an offer of employment (W-

---

[43] United States Department of Agriculture Economic Research Service. "Immigration and the Rural Workforce." May 2013. http://www.ers.usda.gov/topics/in-the-news/immigration-and-the-rural-workforce.aspx#Hired.

[44] United States Department of Agriculture Economic Research Service (2013).

[45] McKissick, J.C., and S. P. Kane. "An Evaluation of Direct and Indirect Economic Losses Incurred by Georgia Fruit and Vegetable Producers in Spring 2011 – A Preliminary Data Analysis and Summary Working Paper." The University of Georgia Center for Agribusiness and Economic Development. Spring 2011. http://gfvga.org/wp-content/uploads/2011/10/Georgia-Fruit-and-Vegetable-Survey-Analysis-Preliminary-Report-10-6-2011.pdf.

[46] Farm Credit Associations of New York, Background Analysis. "Farm Labor and Immigration Reform: Economic Impact to New York State Agriculture." https://www.farmcrediteast.com/resources-and-reports/community-support/public-policy/~/media/files/news/immigrationfarmlaboranalysisny.ashx.

[47] Calvin, L., and P. Martin. "The U.S. Produce Industry and Labor: Facing the Future in a Global Economy." United States Department of Agriculture Economic Research Service, Economic Research Report Number 106. November 2010. http://www.ers.usda.gov/media/135123/err106.pdf.

[48] American Farm Bureau Federation – Economic Analysis Team. "Impact of Migrant Labor Restrictions on the Agricultural Sector." February 2006. http://www.fb.org/newsroom/nr/nr2006/02-07-06/labor%20study-feb06.pdf.

4). These new visas would be valid for three years and could be renewed once for an additional three years. Current unauthorized agricultural workers would also be eligible for "blue cards," providing temporary legal status and the ability to apply for permanent resident status after five years, and eventually citizenship, if they continue to work in agriculture. According to a USDA simulation of a similar policy, an expanded agriculture temporary-worker program[49] would increase long-run agricultural output by between 0.2 percent and 2.0 percent, depending on the crop, and would increase agricultural exports by between 0.2 percent and 3.2 percent.[50]

All of these benefits are reasons that the American Farm Bureau praised the passage of the bipartisan Senate bill, which President Bob Stallman described as "the first step in reforming our broken immigration system and ensuring agriculture has access to a stable and legal workforce."[51]

Boosting Tourism and Hospitality

Another boost to the economy offered by the Senate immigration bill is increased international travel and tourism. Provisions in the bill will facilitate travel while simultaneously strengthening national security through reforming the Visa Waiver Program, expanding trusted traveler programs, increasing the number of U.S. Customs and Border Protection officers at ports of entry, and permanently authorizing the Corporation for Travel Promotion, among other initiatives. New U.S. Customs and Border Protection officers would strengthen the U.S. economy and promote travel and tourism by reducing growing wait-times for travelers and cargo entering the U.S., which in turn creates more jobs and increases GDP; the addition of 3,500 CBPOs is expected to add over 115,000 new jobs annually and increase GDP by $7 billion. For every 1,000 additional CBPOs added, GDP is expected to grow by $2 billion with over 33,000 new jobs added annually.[52]

Travel and tourism comprise the largest service-export industry in the U.S., setting a record $165.6 billion in exports in 2012 and supporting 7.8 million jobs in 2012.[53] The U.S. Department of Commerce projects international travel to the United States will continue to grow strongly through 2018. Building on a record year in 2012, the volume of international visitors is expected to increase

---

[49] The policy simulation assumes an H-2A expansion that increases foreign-born U.S. farmworkers by about 30,000 in year one; 83,000 in year two; and roughly 90,000 in years three and four. Similarly, S.744 would place an annual cap on new agricultural workers (W-3 and W-4 visa holders) at 112,333.

[50] "Immigration Policy and Its Possible Effects on U.S. Agriculture and the Market for Hired Farm Labor: A Simulation Analysis" (2011) United States Department of Agriculture Economic Research Service, Staff Analysis No. 11-341

[51] Statement by Bob Stallman, President, American Farm Bureau Federation, Regarding Senate Passage of Immigration Reform Legislation. June 27, 2013.http://www.fb.org/index.php?action=newsroom.news&year=2013&file=nr0627.html

[52] Estimates based on underlying analysis in Roberts, Bryan, et al. "The Impact on the U.S. Economy of Changes in Wait Times at Ports of Entry." National Center for Risk and Economic Analysis of Terrorism Events, University of Southern California. April 2013. create.usc.edu/CBP%20Final%20Report.pdf

[53] "Fast Facts: United States Travel and Tourism Industry 2012." International Trade Administration, U.S. Department of Commerce. http://tinet.ita.doc.gov/outreachpages/download_data_table/Fast_Facts_2012.pdf.

by 4.0 percent in 2013.[54] National parks and recreation sites are among the most popular destinations for international travelers. In 2010, 20 percent of all international travelers visited a national park, and from 2002 to 2011, one-tenth of all surveyed national parks visitors were of international origin.[55] As wages rise and middle class populations grow in emerging economies, tourists from China, Brazil, and India are expected to increase by 229 percent, 66 percent, and 43 percent, respectively.[56] Improving ease of travel, without compromising our security, will ensure that the U.S. reaps the benefit of this growth in tourism in the near future.

The broader leisure and hospitality industry – one of the fastest-growing sectors of the United States economy[57] – also stands to benefit significantly from commonsense immigration reform. According to the Bureau of Labor Statistics, the leisure and hospitality industry has consistently added jobs over the past 3 years.[58] These sectors remain a source for robust economic activity and continue to exceed expectations.[59] The nation's accommodation and food service industries rely heavily upon seasonal and temporary workers. And like agriculture, a portion of their current workforce is undocumented. Leaders of these industries have been longtime proponents of legislation that would legalize workers in the U.S. and facilitate the lawful employment of future foreign-born workers. The head of the American Hotel and Lodging Association this year applauded the Senate on behalf of the lodging industry for its bipartisan commitment to immigration reform that "creates jobs, boosts travel and tourism, preserves hoteliers' access to a strong seasonal workforce, and stimulates economic growth."[60]

From California to Wisconsin to Tennessee, many state hospitality and tourism entities have vocalized their support of immigration reform which, in the words of the U.S. Travel Association,

---

[54] "U.S. Commerce Department Forecasts Continued Strong Growth for International Travel to the United States – 203-2018," International Trade Administration, U.S. Department of Commerce. June 10, 2013. http://tinet.ita.doc.gov/view/f-2000-99-001/forecast/Forecast_Summary.pdf.

[55] "National Travel & Tourism Strategy Task Force on Travel & Competitiveness," 2012. http://tinet.ita.doc.gov/pdf/national-travel-and-tourism-strategy.pdf

[56] "U.S. Commerce Department Forecasts Continued Strong Growth for International Travel to the United States – 203-2018," International Trade Administration, U.S. Department of Commerce. June 10, 2013. http://tinet.ita.doc.gov/view/f-2000-99-001/forecast/Forecast_Summary.pdf.

[57] "Travel and Tourism Spending Outpaced Growth in the Overall Economy in the First Quarter of 2013." U.S. Department of Commerce, Bureau of Economic Analysis. June 24, 2013. http://bea.gov/newsreleases/industry/tourism/tournewsrelease.htm

[58] Employment, Hours, and Earnings from the Current Employment Statistics survey (National). http://data.bls.gov/timeseries/CES7000000001

[59] "Summary of Commentary on Current Economic Conditions by Federal Reserve District." The Federal Reserve Beige Book. April 17, 2013. http://www.federalreserve.gov/monetarypolicy/beigebook/beigebook201304.htm.

[60] American Hotel & Lodging Association. "AH&LA Applauds Committee Passage of Immigration Reform Bill." Press release. June 26, 2013. http://www.ahla.com/pressrelease.aspx?id=35524

"will boost America's recovery by delivering jobs and economic growth to communities and businesses nationwide."[61,62]

[61] "Hospitality, agriculture leaders push for immigration reform." WACH Fox News Center. June 13, 2013. http://www.midlandsconnect.com/news/story.aspx?id=909448#.UdIX4PmyCJM; Lump, Ed. "Time for comprehensive immigration reform." June 3, 2013. http://www.jsonline.com/news/opinion/time-for-comprehensive-immigration-reform-b9925312z1-210009901.html; Salinas, Claudia Meléndez. "Local ag, hospitality leaders call for immigration reform." May 14, 2013. http://www.montereyherald.com/news/ci_23220001/local-ag-hospitality-leaders-call-immigration-reform.

[62] U.S. Travel Association. "U.S. Travel Commends Senate Passage of Immigration Bill." Press release. June 27, 2013. http://www.ustravel.org/news/press-releases/us-travel-commends-senate-passage-immigration-bill

VI. Stakeholders and Groups Across the Political Spectrum Agree That Immigration Reform is an Economic Win

John Arensmeyer, Small Business Majority: "Small business owners understand that fixing our country's immigration system will help them foster better workforces, which will bolster their bottom lines and our economy as a whole. Increasing the number of pathways for immigrants to come to this country, stay legally and pay taxes will strengthen our economy and encourage a robust and diversified business sector. ... Everyone benefits when we encourage hard-working immigrants to bring their skillsets to the U.S. and let previously undocumented immigrants legally join our workforce, pay taxes and contribute in a meaningful way to our economy."

Douglas Holtz-Eakin, American Action Forum: "Immigration reform can raise population growth, labor force growth, and thus growth in Gross Domestic Product (GDP). In addition, immigrants have displayed entrepreneurial rates above that of the native born population. New entrepreneurial vigor embodied in new capital and consumer goods can raise the standard of living."

U.S. Chamber of Commerce: "Immigration reform is one of the compelling challenges of our time. The Chamber will continue to utilize its resources and promote support among our members for broad immigration reform because America cannot compete and win in a global economy without the world's best talent, hardest workers, or biggest dreamers."

Rupert Murdoch, Chairman and CEO of News Corporation: "I believe that all Americans should have a vital interest in fixing our broken immigration system so we can continue to compete in the 21st Century global economy. ... [A]merica's future prosperity and security depends on getting our immigration policy right—and doing it quickly."

Grover Norquist, President of Americans for Tax Reform: "Immigration reform will jumpstart America's economy and reduce our national debt."

Center for American Progress: "Providing legal status and citizenship to the 11 million undocumented immigrants living in our country would trigger a significant boost to the U.S. economy over the next 10 years: Immigrants would earn more, consumer more, and consequently the economy as a whole would grow."

Chad Stone, Chief Economist at Center on Budget and Policy Priorities: "Immigration reform will be good for the budget and good for the economy."

Information Technology Industry Council: "Immigration reform is central to America's long-term ability to create new jobs and remain the world's innovation leader. The strong, bipartisan support in the Senate for balanced immigration legislation is a significant step away from old, misguided stereotypes and toward a stronger future for American workers and American communities."

Steve Case, Chairman and CEO of Revolution: "The Senate's bill will attract the world's best entrepreneurs and innovators and be a key ingredient to sustaining America's long-term competitive edge."

Gary Shapiro, President and CEO of the Consumer Electronics Association: "The bill embraces immigration reforms that are much needed to welcome foreign-born entrepreneurs, workers and U.S.-educated immigrants to build American businesses and create domestic jobs."

Association of Public and Land-grant Universities: "[The passage of the Senate bill] marks a major milestone in the effort to comprehensively fix a broken immigration system that has failed many who wish to study at U.S. higher education institutions and those who wish to remain here after they graduate and contribute to our economic growth."

Business Roundtable: "BRT supports comprehensive immigration reform that addresses the status of the more than 10 million foreign individuals living in the United States illegally, provides for more efficient and accurate verification of worker eligibility, and improves legal channels that would allow immigrants to help meet the demand for labor across many economic sectors – including the hospitality, construction, agriculture and high-tech industries. We look forward to working with the President and Congress on sensible solutions to make America more competitive in the world economy."

Partnership for a New American Economy: "There is broad support to modernize our immigration system in a way that helps grow our economy and attract the world's most talented and hardest-working. It's time to move from politics to policy by passing a bipartisan bill that brings an immigration system formed in the 1960s into a 21st century global economy."

Madeline Zavodny, Adjunct Scholar at the American Enterprise Institute: "Targeted changes to immigration policy geared toward admitting more highly educated immigrants and more temporary workers for specific sectors of the economy would help generate the growth, economic opportunity, and new jobs that America needs."

National Council of La Raza: "Our economy will grow, the deficit will shrink, jobs will be created and our taxpaying labor force will expand so that we have more workers contributing to our tax system. All of these positives should demonstrate to lawmakers working on reform that we shouldn't delay passage of an immigration bill which will provide our nation with additional economic benefits."

Richard Trumka, President of the AFL-CIO: "The United States Senate today moved our country a big step closer to building a common sense immigration system that will allow millions of aspiring Americans to become citizens. … There is much that works for working people in the Senate bill. Most of all, it allows people who are American in every way except on paper to come out of the shadows, lift themselves out of poverty and be recognized as contributors to our communities and our country."

SEIU: "Passing commonsense, accountable immigration reform is also about a shared commitment to strengthening our economy. Lifting 11 million undocumented workers out of the underground economy would lift wages for every American while generating billions in additional tax revenue."

Max Richtman, President and CEO of Committee to Protect Social Security and Medicare: "We agree with both the Congressional Budget Office and the Chief Actuary of the Social Security Administration (SSA) that comprehensive immigration reform is good for all Americans. The new members of the national family brought in by this bill will contribute to the growth of the economy and at the same time will help strengthen Social Security."

U.S. Travel Association: "The Senate's passage today of historic immigration reform legislation is a significant step toward strengthening U.S. national security and encouraging more travel to and within the United States. Through a number of travel-friendly provisions, the bill will boost America's recovery by delivering jobs and economic growth to communities and businesses nationwide."

American Council on Education: "As both educators and employers, we appreciate this effort at comprehensive immigration reform and believe it represents an important step toward creating an immigration system with bipartisan support that serves the needs of our country."

Center for American Progress: "This bill will also reap economic benefits whose ripple effects will help improve the economic standing of millions of Americans. It's been a long journey to today's victory, and we have plenty of work ahead in the House, but today's Senate vote solidifies the momentum behind real reform and a brighter future for America. The House of Representatives should act swiftly and deliver similar smart and forward-thinking legislation in the weeks ahead."

American Farm Bureau: "The Senate's passage today of a balanced immigration reform bill that includes a fair and workable farm labor provision is welcomed by America's farmers and ranchers...A comprehensive agricultural labor plan that works for all sectors of agriculture and across all regions of our nation is long overdue. We commend the Senate for addressing this very important issue, which will help ensure the continued success of agriculture in our nation."

National Committee to Preserve Social Security & Medicare: "We agree with both the Congressional Budget Office and the Chief Actuary of the Social Security Administration (SSA) that comprehensive immigration reform is good for all Americans. The new members of the national family brought in by this bill will contribute to the growth of the economy and at the same time will help strengthen Social Security."

National Restaurant Association: "America's restaurants support common-sense immigration reform that meets three key priorities: a clear path to legalization, national implementation of the E-Verify employee verification system that preempts inconsistent state mandates, and increased border security that won't harm legal travel and tourism."

www.ingramcontent.com/pod-product-compliance
Lightning Source LLC
Chambersburg PA
CBHW081245170526
45165CB00009B/3206